BRONX BEATS

Chasing Dreams Under City Lights – A Memoir

LUIS MARTINEZ

TABLE OF CONTENTS

This book is dedicated to Kat, Kay and Chris. Thank you for your love and support all these years and allowing me to chase my dreams and for putting up with me. To Mom and Dad, thank you for your push and encouragement, I am forever grateful.

PREFACE

Every journey in the music business begins with a spark of passion, a melody that resonates deep within the soul. For some, this journey starts in the tender years of youth, where dreams are nurtured against the backdrop of endless possibilities. My path to the music industry, however, took a different course. It began much later in life, when the responsibilities of adulthood weighed heavy, and the echoes of doubt resounded louder than the music in my heart.

Growing up in the South Bronx, music was more than just a favorite song or the sound of my parents' records filling the house on a Saturday afternoon—it was a lifeline. Amidst the chaos and struggle, I found sanctuary in the beats and melodies that defined my surroundings. Music wasn't just something I listened to; it was where I discovered my voice. It was here, in the gritty reality of urban life, that my passion for music was ignited—a flame that burned brightly against the backdrop of adversity. It became my escape, my solace, and eventually, my calling.

As an aspiring artist, the challenges I faced were as formidable as the concrete walls that surrounded me. The Bronx wasn't just my home; it was my proving ground. Every day was a battle against the odds, and every step forward felt like a triumph over the obstacles that stood in my way. Yet, amidst the struggle, I found a lifeline in the pulsating rhythms of Freestyle Dance Music—a genre born from the very heart of the city that shaped me. This music left an indelible mark on my journey, serving not only as the soundtrack of my early days but also as a bridge that carried me from the raw energy of Freestyle Dance to the broader horizons of Pop music. It was a testament to the resilience and adaptability needed to evolve as an artist while chasing dreams in a city that never sleeps.

It wasn't until later in life, when the responsibilities of marriage, fatherhood, and a nine-to-five job began to weigh heavily on me, that I found the courage to fully embrace my passion for music. With my family's hesitant support and a determination that refused to waver, I entered the music industry, prepared to carve out my place in a world notorious for its challenges. The journey was far from easy—it was a rollercoaster of highs and lows, triumphs and setbacks—but it was mine. Through it all, I held onto the belief that music was more than just a career; it was my calling.

Through the pages of this memoir, I invite you to journey alongside me as I navigate the intricate pathways of the music industry. From the humble beginnings of teenage performances in a neighborhood park to the exhilarating highs of recording and performing as an artist on grand stages, and ultimately, to my deep love for producing and writing songs for other artists, guiding them on their own journeys. This is a tale marked by resilience, fueled by unwavering passion, and driven by the relentless pursuit of dreams—a story that embodies the transformative power of music and the indomitable spirit of the human soul.

CHAPTER 1.
PLANTING SEEDS

Legend has it that there was a particular TV commercial that would come on late at night while I was sound asleep in my crib, my sister nestled in her bassinet, and my parents trying to catch a breather in our tiny one-bedroom apartment. It was a Crazy Eddie commercial—if you remember those, you're a true New Yorker. Crazy Eddie was this wild electronics store with a commercial where a barbershop quartet would sing the Crazy Eddie jingle from the bathroom.

I could be deep in sleep, but if that commercial came on, I'd miraculously wake up, stand up in my crib, and stare at the TV in utter fascination. My parents couldn't believe their eyes. They'd watch in amazement as I was completely entranced by the jingle, my tiny body swaying to the beat. My mother always swore it was a sign of what was to come, and looking back, maybe she was right.

I fell in love with music at a young age, back when life was simpler, and everything felt new. I was about ten years old, just a kid in the Bronx, surrounded by the sounds of my father's old Reel-to-Reel player. That machine was like a mystery to me, filling our apartment with the rich, vibrant rhythms of classic

Salsa. I never really understood how it worked, but my dad was super protective of it. We couldn't touch the tape because it would leave fingerprints that might make the songs skip—or at least that's what he told us. I can still remember the thrill of hearing the reels spin and the music fill the room, creating a soundtrack to our daily lives.

This Reel-to-Reel wasn't just any old piece of equipment—it was part of a larger sound system that my dad had painstakingly pieced together over time. The system, which included a powerful amplifier and hefty speakers, was one of his prized possessions. He had acquired it during his time in the army in South Korea. While on leave, he would explore local music shops and befriended the owner of one, eventually buying the components piece by piece and shipping them back to the States until he had the complete setup.

Dad's dedication to building that sound system was impressive. He'd talk about how he saved up every spare penny and went without just to get the next piece. The care he took in selecting each component was a testament to his love for music, and it wasn't just about having the best equipment—it was about having something that brought him joy and connected him to a part of his life that he cherished deeply.

Once Dad returned from his service, he'd set up the recorder to capture his favorite New York DJ, El CID, leaving the system to record over seven hours of music. When he got home from work, he'd sift through the recordings, keeping only the parts he wanted and transferring them from one reel to another. It sounds complicated, but a few years later, I found myself doing something similar with my double tape deck boom box. Waiting all night for the hot new song to come on the radio so I could record it became a ritual—something I bet many of you can relate to. That sense of anticipation and excitement was something we both cherished, and it's a memory that still makes me smile.

I can still picture those Saturday mornings vividly. My parents would be busy cleaning the apartment while my father was completely immersed in the music of the Fania All-Stars, Hector Lavoe, Oscar D'León, and Joe Arroyo. Their music wasn't just background noise; it was the heartbeat of our home, a constant reminder of the passion and rhythm that defined our lives. Latin music had an infectious rhythm where the baseline drove the dance, and you had to be in tune with it to catch it. My father played his music loud, and my parents would dance like there was no tomorrow. I didn't understand the words, but I felt the drums and remember the sound of the horns. Looking back, that was the best time in Latin music; it was new to the New York scene and in its infancy.

My father and mother met while they were both in a family band. My dad played the bongos, and my mom sang lead on one of the band's most requested songs. My father once told me that when she sang, he'd get so distracted and mesmerized by her voice that he'd lose the rhythm of the bongos and end up messing up the song. That's just the kind of magic she brought to the stage. Even today, my mom still has a beautiful voice and can definitely still sing—that's where I get my talent from, no doubt about it. My dad, well, he's okay and can hold a tune, but he was always more of a rhythm guy.

The first time I ever heard him sing was on a recording he made during a visit to a theme park in Pennsylvania. Back then, some parks had these karaoke studios where you could pick from a list of songs and record a demo while visiting the park. He chose "On the Road Again" by Willie Nelson, and he sounded so cool. I always remembered that and wish I could find those recordings again.

But if there's one thing you should know about my dad, it's that Salsa was, and still is, his true love. Ask him about music today, and he'll tell you that the new stuff, even artists like Marc Anthony, isn't real Salsa. To him, Salsa is those amazing bands from back in the day, when the recordings were live and raw, with every musician pouring their heart into the performance. It's a sound and an era that he holds dear, something he believes can't be replicated today, no matter how advanced music production has become. But that's a topic for another chapter—one that dives deep into what it means to make music with soul.

But it wasn't just Salsa that filled our lives. Friday nights were something special too. My mom would host her friends, and our living room would transform into a little slice of R&B heaven. The voices of Anita Baker and Luther Vandross would pour out of the speakers, wrapping us in their warmth. My mother loved her soul music, and it was more than just entertainment; it was an education. She'd play everything, from classical to songs in languages I didn't understand, always telling us, "I want you to be exposed to more than what you hear on the radio." Looking back, I realize she was laying the foundation for my love of music, giving me a broad palette to draw from.

My sister and I had our own little musical world too. We'd spend hours with our favorite record, The Sesame Street Monsters! A Musical Monster-Osity. We had this simple box record player—nothing fancy, but it got the job done. We'd cue up our favorite song, "Be Kind to the Monsters in Your Neighborhood," and put a penny on top of the needle to keep it from skipping. Then, we'd dance around our shared bedroom like we were putting on a concert. Sometimes, we'd get brave and ask Mom if we could perform for her and her friends. Marching around the living room, banging on pots and pans, belting out our song, it felt like we were stars for those few minutes. Music was my escape, even then. Performing was my thing; I loved putting on a show. I still remember a routine my sister and I put together to the very popular song "Sube a Mi Moto" by Menudo, only the biggest Latin boy band on the planet at the time. We'd flip our plastic swivel chairs and push them around our room like motorcycles. Now, my sister, bless her heart, might not have had the rhythm or the voice, but she gave it her all. It's a miracle we didn't end up crashing those "motorcycles" with her leading the charge!

Growing up in Lambert Houses in The Bronx had its perks. The neighbors all knew each other, and while that meant there wasn't much we could get away with, it also meant that music was everywhere. The community vibe, the shared experiences—it all revolved around sound. It wasn't unusual to hear all sorts of music blaring from different apartments down the halls from ours. Salsa rhythms mixed with R&B beats, and sometimes, you'd even catch the latest hits playing from someone's radio. I remember that Hip Hop wasn't on the radio yet because I recall the explosion of Sugarhill Gang's "Rapper's

Delight" when my uncle first bought me the record. I was in third grade then, so that was a few years later. For me, music became more than just something to listen to—it was a way to connect, to express, and to feel.

Music wasn't just background noise; it was the heartbeat of our block and something a little more serious in my family. My uncle, my dad's youngest and only brother, was a Hip Hop DJ in Lambert Houses in the Bronx. He was growing up in the Hip Hop movement while I was just getting exposed to music. Lambert Houses was a mecca for Hip Hop, birthing some of the legends in the genre. Grandmaster Flash, Grandmaster Caz, members of the Furious Five, and Kid Creole could often be found hanging around the block and throwing jams across the street in Bronx Park.

I was too young to remember much, but my uncle was in the thick of it and shared many stories with me. He lived with my grandparents, and I remember that when visiting their house, I could hear music coming from his room. The times he let me in, it felt like stepping into a different world. His bedroom had a futon and a small dresser on one side, and a long DJ table with two turntables, speakers, and a mixer. Underneath the table, he had quite a few milk crates filled with records. I would spend hours just looking at album covers in amazement—until he caught me and threw me out of his room.

In hindsight, it feels like I was being groomed, prepared for what was to come. I don't remember if I had a voice yet during those early years, and I don't even think I had a conscious desire to be a singer. But what I do remember is being deeply connected to music. I was knowledgeable about it at a very young age. I knew artists' names, I knew what a music genre was, I knew what a chorus and a verse were. I remembered song titles and started associating how certain songs made me feel.

And then there was that one song, the one that always had a way of cutting through everything else, grabbing my attention no matter what I was doing. My mother has it on repeat and I remember how the song started, like someone reading a letter. The song was "Kiss and Say Goodbye" by The Manhattans. Every time my mom played it, everything would slow down. I remember it being very sad and would make me feel sorry for the lady this man was singing to, like why would he leave? It was one of the first times I realized that music wasn't just something you heard—it was something you felt deep inside.

A few years ago, my mother and I took a road trip to Georgia. Just the two of us, driving seven hours from Florida to see one of her old friends—one of those close friends who used to spend Friday nights at our house, listening to music. We spent the entire trip the same way we used to spend those evenings—laughing, reminiscing, and of course, listening to music. She was surprised by how many of the songs I remembered, but I wasn't. Those songs were etched into my memory, woven into the fabric of who I am. My mother has always been supportive of me and has always been my biggest fan. Whenever I get the chance, I remind her of that—how important the roots she planted more than 40 years ago have been in shaping who I am today.

BRONX BEATS

CHAPTER 2.
BRONX BEATS

B y the time I reached my teenage years, I was no longer just a listener of music—I was becoming a seeker of it. My father's reel-to-reel tapes and my mother's soulful records had set the foundation, but now, I was ready to find my own sound. The Bronx was alive with energy, and I could feel the pulse of the city, almost as if the concrete itself had a rhythm. It wasn't just the Salsa, R&B, and Motown that had filled our apartment for so many years; it was something different, something new, and it called to me.

Growing up in the Lambert Houses projects, Hip Hop wasn't just music—it was a lifestyle, a culture, and for me, a lifeline. The Bronx was the birthplace of Hip Hop, and living there meant that this new wave of music was in the air, on the streets, and in our homes. I was in my early teens when Hip Hop started to shape my world. It wasn't just about the beats and the rhymes; it was about how we dressed, how we talked, and how we moved through life.

I remember the thrill of staying up late to catch DJ Red Alert and DJ Marley Marl on the radio, fingers hovering over the record button on my double tape deck boombox, ready to capture their latest mixes. Those nights were electric—when you caught that perfect mix or that new track everyone was buzzing about, it was like striking gold. My friends and I would trade these tapes like they were treasures, each one a piece of the culture that was growing around us.

Hip Hop was more than music; it was a movement. We weren't just passive consumers; we were participants, co-creators in a culture that was being built from the ground up. The artists of that time were our leaders, our storytellers. Eric B. & Rakim, Big Daddy Kane, Slick Rick, MC Lyte, BDP, A Tribe Called Quest, Jungle Brothers, Leaders of the New School—these were the voices that narrated our lives. Their lyrics were more than just words; they were mantras we lived by.

I can still recall the rush I felt when a DJ threw on "Eric B. for President" at a house party. The moment Rakim's voice cut through the speakers with, "I came through the door, I said it before, I never let the mic magnetize me no more," the entire room would erupt. The energy was contagious, and in those moments, it felt like we were part of something bigger, something powerful. The bass would shake the walls, and the crowd would move as one, lost in the rhythm, in the words, in the message that Hip Hop was delivering. It was more than music—it was a declaration of who we were, where we came from, and where we were going.

One of my closest friends, DJ Serious Cee, was my guide into the world of DJing. He was the one who introduced me to the art of record selection and blending. He had a gift for reading the crowd, knowing exactly what they needed to hear to keep the vibe alive. We'd spend hours in his room, crates of records surrounding us, experimenting with different mixes, trying to create that perfect sound. I was fascinated by the way he could take two seemingly unrelated tracks and blend them into something entirely new, something that made the room light up. The way he could manipulate sound, creating a mood, a feeling, with just a few turns of the vinyl—it was magic to me. And I wanted to learn every bit of it.

As my love for Hip Hop deepened, I began to express myself through it. I started writing my own rhymes, filling notebooks with verses, trying to emulate the flow and wordplay of the greats. I wasn't just copying them—I was finding my own voice, my own style. I had bags full of cassettes, each one a testament to my love for Hip Hop. It wasn't just a phase or a trend; it was a part of me, woven into the fabric of my identity. I can still remember the pride I felt when I strung together a verse that had the right rhythm, the right punch. It was like discovering a new part of myself, a part that had been waiting to be unleashed.

Here's a little sample of one of my early rhymes:

"From the highest mountain to the deepest sea
If you want to battle him, you gotta battle me
'Cause my name is L Ski in the place to be
And I'll rock your whole university
I'm potentially inclined, the mastermind
Tough enough to bust up all of your rhymes
So I'll give you L Ski, which is my mission
Come to battle me, it's like no competition
Like the summer shine in the summertime
I don't do no crime, all I do is rhyme

So yeah, my name is L Ski, and I put you to the test
But everybody knows, that I'm the best"

These lines, scrawled in a notebook with frayed edges, were more than just words—they were a declaration of my place in this world, a world shaped by the streets of the Bronx, the beats of Hip Hop, and the dreams that were growing inside me.

It was the early '80s, and the Bronx was experiencing a musical revolution. Everywhere I turned, there was a sense of change in the air—on street corners, in parks, at block parties, you could hear it. Hip Hop was exploding, of course, but there was also another sound creeping into the mix, something that resonated with me on a deeper level: Freestyle Dance. The genre was still in its infancy, but it was unmistakable—the blend of Latin beats, electronic sounds, and soulful melodies created a vibe that was entirely fresh and unique. It was the sound of a new generation, and I wanted to be part of it. Freestyle was primarily performed by Latin artists—people who lived in the same communities I did, who looked like me, who shared the same stories. It was music that felt like it belonged to us.

I remember the first time I really heard Freestyle. It wasn't just music; it was an experience. I was at a local record store—yeah, we had record stores back in our time, and those places were like sanctuaries for us, a place that became a second home to me during those years—when I heard the track "Let the Music Play" by Shannon. The moment the beat dropped, it was like my world shifted. For me, it was like a mixture of Hip Hop and Dance but with singing on top of it, and it was ours.

Artists like Judy Torres, Coro, George LaMond, Cynthia, Johnny O, Exposé, TKA—they shaped the Freestyle sound. I had their posters plastered on my bedroom walls; their cassette albums lined up in perfect order. Freestyle was different; it wasn't just about listening; it was about moving. You could dance to it, create routines, and lose yourself in the rhythm. And it wasn't just Freestyle—Freestyle House was on the rise too, with groups like 2 Without Hats and 2 in a Room leading the charge. The music was infectious, filled with energy, emotion, and a sense of freedom that spoke directly to my soul.

I was in high school when I met Kashim from 2 Without Hats. We both went to Cardinal Hayes High School in the Bronx. But I'll get into that a little later in the book. Meeting him made me feel even more connected to the music, like this wasn't just a genre—it was part of who I was becoming. The fact that someone from my own high school was part of this movement made it feel even more real, more attainable. It wasn't just about listening to the music anymore; it was about being part of it, about contributing to a culture that was growing and evolving every day.

Finally, I had music that felt like it was mine, something that represented my culture, my experiences. I was still too young to get into the clubs where my favorite Freestyle artists performed, but that didn't matter. I was incredibly lucky, and if you're wondering why, let me tell you.

Sparkle Productions was the premier artist management company in the Bronx, managing the biggest stars in Freestyle Dance music. The queen herself, Judy Torres, along with Johnny O, Suave, Exposé—they were all part of the Sparkle roster. And guess what? My uncle worked for Sparkle Productions under George Vascones (may he rest in peace) as one of their road managers. My aunt was the staff secretary at the Grand Concourse office, and my dad was their bookkeeper. So yeah, you could say I was connected.

I had full access to the movement and the stars. I got to hear demos before they were even recorded, attend rehearsals, and sit in on studio sessions. I rolled in limos to and from shows—except for the club venues, of course. I had a front-row seat to an exploding genre, and I soaked up every moment of it. That's when I caught the bug, the one that's been with me ever since. Freestyle wasn't just music to me—it was the spark that ignited my passion for creating, performing, and living within the world of music.

I remember this one time when Johnny O was having his record release party at a club venue, and it was the place to be. I was 16 or 17 at the time. My aunt instructed my dad to dress me up to look older, so I had to wear a suit and tie, and I remember my dad lending me some of his jewelry. I rolled into the venue with the team and managed to get away with it. That night, a young artist by the name of Lil Suzy was making her premiere performance. She was tiny, just a kid, but she already had a smash hit with "Take Me in Your Arms." I think that moment solidified it for me—I knew then what I wanted to do. I wanted to sing, perform, write songs—I wanted to be a star.

It was around this time that I also started to take my passion for songwriting seriously. Freestyle was the backdrop, but my writing wasn't limited to just one genre. I wrote what I felt, what I saw, and what I wanted to express. The music wasn't just about beats and rhythms; it was about telling a story, painting a picture with words. Every song I wrote was a piece of me, a glimpse into my world, and I poured everything I had into those lyrics. I wanted to create something that resonated with others the way Hip Hop and Freestyle resonated with me.

As the years went on, I continued to write, to create, to explore. Music had become more than just a passion—it was my identity, my purpose. I knew I was destined for something bigger, something beyond the boundaries of the Bronx. I wanted to take everything I had learned, everything I had experienced, and put it into my music. My journey was just beginning, and I was ready to dive in headfirst, to embrace the unknown, and to find my voice.

CHAPTER 3.
FINDING MY VOICE

Falling in love with music is easy, but pursuing success in it? That's a whole different story. The questions that haunt you—Do you have the talent? The drive? Can you handle rejection?—linger throughout your journey. Even now, those questions still echo in my mind. The music business is full of highs and lows, and it's no wonder so many aspiring artists never make it out of their bedrooms. Or do they?

Back in the early '90s, the music industry was a fortress guarded by gatekeepers—managers, entertainment lawyers, and record company A&Rs (Artists and Repertoire). These were the people who decided which artists had the potential to make it and which ones would never get past the front door. It wasn't enough just to have talent; you had to navigate a maze of industry insiders who held the keys to your success. Getting your music into the hands of the right person was an uphill battle, often filled with rejection and frustration. You had to be persistent, knocking on doors and hoping someone would take a chance on you. This was a time when demo tapes were passed around like secret treasures, and if one of these gatekeepers didn't like what they heard, your music would never see the light of day.

Unlike today, where artists can upload a song online and instantly reach a global audience, back then, it was a different game. There was no YouTube, no TikTok, no social media to showcase your talent. The gatekeepers controlled access to the public, and without their approval, you were stuck performing at local shows, hoping for a break.

When I first started discovering my talent, I was around 14 or 15, just starting high school. I knew I loved to write and sing, and although I had access to some support and a few willing listeners, I didn't have the means to record my music. Back then, recording a demo was limited to paying for a quick karaoke session at Great Adventure or begging a DJ friend to record you singing over a beat they'd mixed.

I practiced constantly, singing some of my favorite songs and recording myself over and over again on my boombox. Occasionally, I was brave enough to let my mom hear my songs or sing for her in my bedroom. Other times, I'd muster up more courage and take my music to my uncle, only to be met with rejection. Eventually, I figured I needed some help. So, I put together my first group, "Images of Time." One of the members Alex was a close friend from high school, and the other was his good friend, Jose. We began performing covers of songs from one of my favorite Freestyle groups, Quadlibet, who were signed to Sparkle Productions at the time—a label I had access to through family connections.

Images of Time performed anywhere and everywhere we could—from neighborhood block parties to sweet sixteens. I remember one show where my aunt managed to get us a limo, and I asked my dad to road-manage us. That night, I think I surprised him. I remember him saying he was shocked to see I had that kind of talent. In hindsight, these moments were my training ground—where I learned how to perform, execute routines, sing, and write songs.

It was during one of these shows that I met my future wife. It was my sister's Ring Day party at our local community center. My sister and my soon-to-be wife's little sister were classmates, and my wife had been invited to chaperone her sister to the party. Of course, I barged into my sister's party planning to make sure she included my group in the lineup. I walked in wearing a black blazer, white tee, blue jean shorts, and platform shoes, ready to take the stage with my guys. We did our thing, and that's when I laid eyes on her—my future wife. It was 1991. I was a senior in high school, and she was a freshman in college. But more on that love story later.

I spent most of high school as part of Images of Time, and eventually, I became known as "Freestyle Lou." Images of Time disbanded after high school graduation for no other reason than change in times, but we remain friends today. I was surrounded by a lot of talent during those years, most of my friends were singers and DJs. Some of them have gone on to make names for themselves in the music business today, like my boy DJ Lucho, who is now a well-known DJ in the industry.

But it wasn't until I graduated from high school that I truly started finding my voice. In 1993, just a few months after graduation, I got a call from an old high school friend. He knew I could sing and perform, and he was looking for a partner to form a group. He had a plan to record a demo and walk it into a popular new freestyle music label at the time, Artistik Records. You see, Freestyle Music in 1993 was taking a backseat to Hip Hop and Grunge Rock. Major New York radio stations like Hot 97 and KTU 103.5 weren't playing Freestyle Music like they used to, and many would say this was the beginning of the end for Freestyle as we knew it. But there was a new sound emerging, underground—meaning it wasn't played on mainstream radio, but there was still a dedicated fanbase craving Freestyle. This sound would eventually be known as New School Freestyle, and it found roots in places like Massachusetts, Connecticut, New York, Texas, Florida, and California.

We formed our group, "On2," and hit the studio for the first time and it would be my first time professionally recording a demo. I was nervous as hell, but it would be first experience hearing a song that I wrote on a piece of paper come to life. I'll never forget walking into that space, the walls lined with soundproof padding, the massive mixing console covered in dials and switches, the glow of the studio lights reflecting off the equipment. It was like stepping into another world—a world that I had only imagined in my dreams. But this wasn't just any visit; we were on the clock, paying for studio time, which meant every second counted. The pressure was on, and it was daunting, especially for a first-timer like me.

I remember how nervous I was, hands sweating, my heart racing as I stood in front of that microphone, staring at the pop filter. This was it. This was the moment where all my scribbled notes and melodies had to come together. We had to be efficient—no time for mistakes or second-guessing. I could feel the weight of the moment, the ticking of the clock pushing us forward. But at the same time, I was captivated by the process. The sheer amount of equipment, the complexity of the soundboard, the way the producer expertly adjusted levels and EQ—it all piqued my curiosity. I wanted to know everything—how it worked, what each button did, how to make a track sound polished and professional.

And then came the moment of truth: hearing my voice recorded for the first time. It was surreal, like an out-of-body experience. There's something almost magical about hearing yourself through the speakers, with every nuance and inflection amplified. It was a mix of awe and disbelief. That was me—that was my voice, my song, coming through those speakers. It was more than just a playback; it was a validation of everything I'd been working towards. I knew I had a lot to learn, but in that moment, I also knew I had something real, something worth pursuing.

We then took that demo and shopped for a deal and ended up at the doors of Artistik Recordings. This label was very popular and just starting to make an impact on the newly crowned genre of New School Freestyle, many would argue that its probably the top label in the genre, even today. We met with label owner Willie and let him hear our song and he loved it. He was building additional record labels at the time and we would go on to premiere on his newest label AVP Records. We were one song on a compilation of artist and the compilation dropped in 1994.

When I learned that the record was released, I made my way to 42nd Street in New York City, hopping on the train with butterflies in my stomach. I headed straight for Times Square to the famous Virgin Megastore. I walked in, made my way to the dance music section, and started shuffling through the CDs. There it was—a compilation with a little photo of On2 on the cover among the other artists. I can't explain the feeling, but it was incredible. This was just the beginning.

On2 went on to record many more singles and appear on several more AVP Records compilations. As a singer and songwriter, I grew more confident and experienced. My partner in On2 was more involved in the business side of things and eventually partnered with the label, while I handled most of the songwriting, vocal arrangements, and managing our studio sessions. I was learning so much back then, and I'm forever grateful to Willie for his trust and guidance. His studio became my second home. We had a lot of fun, just doing what we loved.

During this time, I met and befriended one of my closest friends today, who was also one of my musical heroes. In 1995, I met Aby at a freestyle show. Aby is the original "A" in the legendary Freestyle group TKA.

Freestyle group TKA will forever be remembered as one of the greatest Freestyle groups of all time. They weren't just another group; they were the blueprint, the gold standard that everyone in the genre aspired to emulate. Their songs were anthems that defined a generation, and their influence reached far beyond the New York City clubs where they first made a name for themselves. For me, as a young aspiring artist, TKA represented everything I wanted to be. Their music wasn't just catchy—it was the soundtrack to our lives. Tracks like "Maria," "One Way Love," and "Louder Than Love" were more than just songs; they were cultural milestones that captured the essence of what it meant to be young and passionate in the 80s and 90s. They showed me that it was possible to come from the same streets I did and make a mark on the world through music.

What's even more amazing is that many years later, I would come full circle, working directly with all the members of TKA on some of their projects. It's surreal to think that the very group that inspired me as a young artist, the legends I idolized, are now my collaborators and peers. It's a testament to the lasting impact of Freestyle music and how it continues to bring people together, even decades after its supposed decline.

On2 was the opening act for one of these shows, and that's how Aby and I crossed paths. We talked for hours that night, just getting to know each other. Man, I had so many questions for him. I was speaking to one of my musical heroes, a legend. But what struck me most was how humble and open he was. That night would mark the beginning of a 30-year friendship. Aby is one of my mentors; he's the person I bounce all my songs and ideas off of. He is my "No" guy, the one who tells me the truth about my music, but he is also one of my best friends. Aby would go on to become a road manager for Strange WayZ, which we'll discuss more in the next chapter, and help shape my career. Go grab some coffee; this one is going to be a doozy!

LUIS MARTINEZ

CHAPTER 4.
MOMMA I MADE IT

My run with On2 and freestyle music came to an end in late 1995 when I discovered a new love: pop music. This was during the boy band craze, with acts like The Backstreet Boys, *NSYNC, and 98 Degrees, as well as iconic female artists like Britney Spears and Christina Aguilera dominating the airwaves. I had always been a pop songwriter, even before my days with On2, and that love for catchy pop melodies and hooks set me apart from most of my peers. One of my later group partners used to refer to me as "the poppiest mother %@! I know," and he wasn't wrong. Writing pop music came naturally to me, so when I heard songs like "Quit Playing Games" and "I Want It That Way," it just clicked. That was exactly what I wanted to do, so I switched gears.

During my time with On2, I had the opportunity to meet and work with several producers, so I already had connections to help me create my new sound. I reached out to another good friend of mine in the industry, Angel Love, the other "A" of TKA. Angel had replaced Aby in TKA in the late '80s. Although we didn't immediately click when we first met, he turned out to be a great friend, and we've worked together a lot since. He was my ride to the studio in Connecticut where I recorded my first pop song, and man, was it a doozy. The song was titled "Dreaming," and it would catapult me into countless opportunities and open so many doors—but more on that later.

When we arrived at the studio, we got straight to work, transforming my idea into a bona fide pop hit. I can say that now, but at the time, the song took a lot of turns. I recorded the leads, Angel sang the B-section, and we collaborated on the hook. The icing on the cake was when the producer, and long-time friend, Edwin "Eddie Ed" Ramos, brought in a guitarist to lay down his contribution. The song came to life. "Dreaming" is by far one of my favorite songs in my catalog to this day.

The song tells the story of a girl struggling with mental health who ultimately takes her own life, leaving me dreaming about the day we would reunite. I know it's a sad story, but unless you really paid attention to the lyrics, you probably wouldn't pick up on it right away. The melody was the driver—it was infectious and easy to follow, one of the key ingredients of pop music.

Verse: I see your eyes
They look away
Wondering tonight if you'll stay
Where have you been, girl
All of my life
There is so much I must say
How much I love
How much I care
Can't live without you
Will you always be there

Chorus: I'll be dreaming
The day that I fall in love, forever
Can we make it last, only together
Forever
Forever

Verse: The light in your eyes
Brightens my skies
No rain in those clouds for all days
Could I have been wrong
To think you were fine
Days pass us by, now you're gone
Oh, heavens await you
We live our own lives
Could I have saved you
From the pain deep inside

I now had my first real pop record and did what any aspiring recording artist would do at the time—I shopped for a deal. I remember walking into Robbins Entertainment, a pop dance record label that was home to acts like Cascada and Rockell. I pitched my demo and they loved the song but felt there wasn't a market for a latino soloist in pop music. It was a sign of the times, because just a few years later, we would experience the "Latin Explosion" with artists like Marc Anthony, Ricky Martin, and Jennifer Lopez—but I digress. Maybe I just wasn't ready yet.

In 1997, I landed the opportunity of a lifetime thanks to my old freestyle connections. My partner from On2 and our producer, Willie Valentin, were working with a local promoter doing radio spots for shows they were promoting. It just so happened that they were promoting a concert at the famous Apollo Theater in New York, featuring Chico DeBarge. He was a member of the uber-famous DeBarge family from the '80s and was a big box office draw. His fans were there to enjoy pop and R&B music—nothing that my former singing partner or producer could offer. But word had gotten around about what I had been doing since leaving On2, so they gave me a call and asked if I would do the show and perform my song "Dreaming" as part of On2. It was a no-brainer for me—are you kidding? Showtime at the Apollo was a legendary show that aired weekly, showcasing amateur artists who performed at the mercy of the relentless, brutally honest Apollo audience. If the first note out of your mouth didn't move the crowd, you were booed off the stage, and the Sandman would come out to gladly escort you off. It was brutal.

But this wasn't amateur night—this was a concert, and we were the opening act. I remember we went all out: we hired a choreographer, found a sponsor to style us with fly gear, and rehearsed like there was no tomorrow. This was the legendary Apollo stage we were talking about. I remember my first time arriving; it's a very old building with dark stairways. I noticed how small it was—the stage was tiny, nothing like it seemed on television. They put us up in a dressing room covered in signatures: the Jacksons, Prince, the Temptations, Smokey Robinson, Luther Vandross, and the list went on and on. We signed our names too, though I was too nervous to remember exactly where, but we were there, too. That was an amazing experience, and I'm proud to say I've performed on that famous stage.

After that, I didn't have much luck finding a deal, so I decided to switch gears. One thing I noticed during the boy band craze was that there weren't any Latino boy bands out at the time. I thought, "Here's my opportunity to fill a void and maybe better my chances of getting signed." I also missed sharing music with brothers-in-arms. It was my safe place, what I knew my entire career up to that point, so I was on the hunt. I mentioned in a previous chapter that many of my friends were already singers and DJs, so it was easy to put a group together. I spent years just hanging out with them, learning how to sing in a group and mastering harmonies. One group was on the rise from around the way—they called themselves Mi Mayor. I was super close with one of the lead singers, as we grew up in the same neighborhood. Mi Mayor was awesome, but they sang primarily in Spanish. Around the same time, I joined On2, I was approached by Alex to audition for Mi Mayor, but back then, I was too tall and had put on too much weight—go figure.

I reached out to one of my childhood friends, Paris, to see if he was interested in forming a group with me. He said yes, but the boy band formula called for 4-5 members, so we kept searching. I then contacted another mutual friend, CL, who reached out to his good friend Dee. I knew Dee because, back in my Images of Time days, he was in a group that was in direct competition with us for the ladies' attention. We can laugh about it now, but back then, I hated his guts. And so, we found our four members, and Strange WayZ was formed.

The first order of business was to get these guys in the studio to re-record "Dreaming." It would go on to be our signature song. Paris and I shared the lead vocals, while CL and

Dee blessed the track with their harmonies. This time, we decided to hold off on shopping for a deal and instead focused on honing our show and building our catalog. We needed to learn each other, build our brotherhood, take our lumps, and earn our spot in the industry.

We had a lot of success between 1999 and 2001. Our first big break was landing the gig as the Opening Act for the 98 Degrees and Rising Tour. Yes, a major pop tour, performing in stadiums. During this time, we had gotten pretty popular in New York and caught the attention of a great manager who worked for ICM (International Creative Management), one of the leading booking agents in New York City. An opportunity came up for a tour they were managing, and they needed an opening act to take over the last leg of the 98 Degrees tour. 98 Degrees, who were signed to Motown, were right up there in popularity with Backstreet Boys and *NSYNC. This was huge for a four-guy group from the hood, but we were up for the task. We escalated our rehearsal schedule to prep for the tour and joined 98 Degrees in Pennsylvania.

On our first night on tour, we performed in a theater that held about 4,000 seats. I remember when they rushed us to stage left, handed us four cordless mics, the house lights dropped, and the crowd went deafening. Imagine 4,000 girls all screaming at the same time—it was surreal. We rushed to our marks on the stage, and when the spotlights hit us, it was bananas. We were off to the races. What a night and what a first-time experience! We did several other shows on the tour, ending with our last performance in a stadium with over 10,000 screaming fans. Strange WayZ was on our way!

Just a few months later, another unique opportunity crossed our doorstep. We were asked to submit a video tape and audition for a Disney Channel TV series called 2 Hour Tour, which was coming to New York to film. It was an opportunity to be paired up with global superstar Enrique Iglesias. We were tasked with recording a video for Enrique, demonstrating why we should be picked to tour with him, which included our music. A few weeks later, we heard back from the production company and were told that we were selected as one of three finalists and that we would appear on the show as a result. The show was the final audition, where we were up against two other artists. If we won, we would spend a few days with Enrique and end with performing as his opening act at the Copa Cabana.

We won!

What followed was nothing short of miraculous for some city kids who started out with nothing but a dream. The audition was part of the show's formula—if you were selected, you'd go on a whirlwind media blitz with Enrique Iglesias, leading up to the final show. But before we even got to that point, we did something unplanned that ended up making a huge impact on our fans and supporters.

For the show taping, we decided to wear matching outfits: blue jeans, windbreaker jackets, and Timbs. We picked this outfit without giving much thought to it, not realizing that we were dressing like quintessential New Yorkers. We were rocking the "hood" uniform—not because we planned it, but because it was just who we were. Later, we were told by multiple fans, supporters, and friends that we repped our hood that day. We weren't shy or ashamed of who we were or where we came from. Picture it: a Disney show featuring four Latino men, dressed in jeans and Timbs, singing pop music. In hindsight, it was brilliant. Perhaps that authenticity is what put us over the top.

After winning the competition, we were whisked off the set and straight to MTV's TRL. Man, oh man! We got to hang with Carson Daly during a live taping, stand in the infamous window overlooking Times Square, and wave at our fans—or rather, Enrique's fans. It was a surreal experience. That evening, we parted ways with Enrique but were expected back on set the following day.

The next day was action-packed. We started with a visit to a Manhattan school, where we met with students alongside Enrique. The session, hosted by the Grammys, had us sitting in the back of the classroom as Enrique fielded questions from the students. Afterward, we headed to one of our favorite radio stations, KTU 103.5, for a live on-air interview with Enrique. The DJ, Broadway Billy, was incredibly cool and welcoming. He even let us share the mic with Enrique. The craziest part? Broadway asked if he could play our song live on the air. What? On KTU? The station we grew up listening to? After a resounding yes, we sat there, listening to our voices live over New York's radio waves, with Enrique in our corner cheering us on. It was another surreal experience.

We finished the night with rehearsals alongside Enrique, preparing for the big show. We had the chance to spend some quality time with him, soaking in his advice and stories. He was humble, accommodating, and genuinely interested in our journey. Over those few days, we grew close and considered him a friend. I stayed in touch with Enrique for a few months after, but we eventually lost contact as his career exploded. Still, we were proud to have been a small part of his musical journey.

The night of the Copa Cabana show was electric. We had our own trailer at the back of the club and were buzzing with excitement. What you probably won't see on the TV show, but everyone on set experienced, is that we had to perform our songs multiple times so the film crew could capture all the footage they needed. It was strange for a live concert, but that's just part of the filming process. After the show, we said our goodbyes and thanked Enrique for the opportunity and for believing in us. We headed back to the hotel for more filming to recap the show. If you look closely at the episode, you'll see at one point I'm closing my eyes during the final group interview—lol, it was 4 a.m., for God's sake!

The best part of this whole experience? Our episode aired on the Disney Channel on repeat daily for three months. You can't get better exposure than that! You can find the whole episode, condensed without commercials, on YouTube by searching "Strange WayZ on Disney." Go check it out!

This appearance and what happened on the show catapulted our career. We were featured in multiple teen magazines like Teen People and Teen Beat, and appeared on several entertainment news shows like Inside Edition and Real Access. Things were getting serious fast. We were signed to Hollywood Records for a while as we navigated the media blitz. It was an amazing ride that ended in 2001. You see, we started our journey at the very tail end of the boy band craze and ended our career at the close of the Latin Explosion. There was no longer a demand for what we were offering, and the label eventually dropped us, marking the end of the Strange WayZ run.

I always boast that out of all our friends in music at the time, we were probably the most successful. Mi Mayor was right there alongside us, but in the Latin market. It was a great run, one that I am very proud of. TV, radio, tours, stadiums, national magazines—yeah, we did that.

CHAPTER 5.
WHAT THE MUSIC BUSINESS IS REALLY LIKE

Shortly after being dropped from our label, we made a few changes to the team around us, starting with management. This change turned out to be both a blessing and a curse, which I'll explain later. Our previous manager, Big George, was a wonderful person—he genuinely loved us and wanted the best for us. He was well-connected and the one who got us on tour with 98 Degrees. George worked for ICM (International Creative Management), one of the top booking agencies in New York City, and we spent a lot of time in their offices on Park Avenue during that period. That's where we recorded many of our media interviews after the Disney Special had aired, including our Teen People magazine interview. One of the guys couldn't make it that day, and I remember Paris filling in for both his voice and CL's—it was hilarious to us. ICM was great to us, but change was inevitable.

The management change happened shortly after our Disney special aired. We were actively being pursued by another manager, Roman, who had experience managing urban, Latino groups like ours. Roman managed a group called Voz, which had seen a lot of success, and that caught our attention. Roman started showing up at our shows, and sometimes it felt like we were cheating on George. But Roman talked a good game, sold us a dream, and—most importantly—a plan. He was blunt, brutally honest, and didn't sugarcoat anything. He called out our flaws and told us the truth about our sound, image, and the type of music we were performing. It was a tough pill to swallow, but we ended up signing with him.

Roman came through on one of his promises by getting us signed to a production deal. It was our first real deal where someone decided to put their money where their mouth was. We were now being invested in, but with that investment came a loss of control—that's the curse I was talking about earlier. Welcome to the real music business. Our producer, George, had a studio in Jersey City, NJ, which became our second home. His engineer, Jake, handled all our sessions, and we were being coached during every recording. Up until this point, we had financed our own studio time, called the shots on our songs, and controlled every aspect of our recording process. But now, that control was gone.

Between Roman, George, and Jake, we were being directed and guided, which slowly chipped away at the core of Strange WayZ. We came into the deal as a pop group, but times had changed, and there wasn't much appetite for four Latinos from the Bronx singing pop anymore. Paris and I sang most of the leads, while CL and Dee handled background vocals and spoken parts. But as we began recording new tracks, it felt like we were being separated. Roman arranged studio sessions for Paris and me without the other two guys, and one day, he even invited a featured artist to record and shut the group out of the session entirely. I should have seen the signs then, but more trouble was on the horizon.

Eventually, CL had a falling out with management and left the group—our first casualty. That hit hard because we had all come into this together, but now we were signed and no longer in control. Dee followed soon after, and before long, Paris and I were the last two standing from the original lineup. In hindsight, we probably should have called it quits then, but the train had already left the station. Roman started auditioning new members, and we cycled through a few. I remember one audition where Roman placed an ad in The Village Voice, and we rented a rehearsal space in the city. This one guy walked in, and although he had the look, the second he started singing, Paris and I had to fight back laughter. We kept searching, though, until we finally met Fredo.

Fredo was talented—a great vocalist, songwriter, and aspiring producer. We clicked immediately. He brought an R&B flavor to the group that we didn't have before and took over as lead singer. It was hard for me to adjust to that change, seeing the group's sound evolve. But not long after, Paris left too, and I was the last original member of Strange WayZ.

As part of our production deal, we were assigned a vocal coach, Gary, one of the best in the business. Gary didn't play around—if you didn't hit your notes, he'd be all over you. It was during these coaching sessions that we met Ray and Victor. These two guys became good friends, and after Paris left, Fredo and I approached Roman and George about bringing them into the group. The catch? We'd have to change the name. That's how ForeKast was born.

ForeKast was a significant shift for me, both musically and vocally. It's where I truly learned the art of harmony, being part of a vocal group where everyone could hold their own. Our sound was full of rich harmonies, upbeat tracks, and catchy hooks. We all contributed to the writing, which led to some friendly competition over whose songs would make it onto our projects. That dynamic changed when we met Jim Beanz—who we affectionately called "Jimba." Early in his career, Jimba was just getting started, but he would go on to become one of the biggest producers in the R&B and hip-hop world, working with the likes of Timbaland, Justin Timberlake, Britney Spears, and many others.

Working with Jimba was an incredible experience. He helped produce some of our best tracks, like "Friends with Privileges," "Too Bad," and "Make It Right." Although those songs were never officially released, they can be found on a mixtape I dropped in 2006 called Love & War: The Mixtape, available as a free download on my website .

Jimba's vocal arrangements were incredible, and he even helped me find my place in the group vocally. In ForeKast, I was no longer the lead singer like I had been in Strange WayZ. Now, we had four lead singers, and everyone could transition between leads and harmonies seamlessly. That was the magic of ForeKast.

As we started building a relationship with Jimba as part of our production team, we also decided to cut ties with Roman, our manager. We felt like we were heading in a new direction and wanted to regain control of our career, so we ended that chapter.

Our recording sessions with Jimba, George, and Jake were a lot of fun. We began experimenting with our vocal arrangements, and for the first time, we had someone who could really sing guide us through the execution. Jimba became my cheerleader, pushing me to reclaim some lead vocal parts and helping me find my voice within this new R&B-focused group dynamic. Fredo, Ray, and Vic were vocal powerhouses— each of them could riff, perform vocal runs, and had amazing control. I came from the pop world, where you could sing a straight melody without much variation. But R&B required something else entirely, and I often felt overshadowed by the others. When Jimba joined the team, he helped me find my place in this new vocal landscape, and for that, I'll always be grateful. He taught me a huge lesson about confidence and versatility.

We had an incredible team with George and Jake. George was our producer, the mastermind behind our sound, and the one who owned the studio where we recorded. He was full of stories, always animated with his raspy voice. I still crack up thinking about the time he told us about a possum he found in his old studio. The way he described it, he said it looked at him, raised its paws like claws, and snarled. George had a habit of saying "No, no, no!" to anything we asked before reconsidering, as if on autopilot. Then he'd ask, "Wait, what was it again?" I miss him dearly—he passed away about 10 years ago due to health complications. I'm not sure what became of the studio in Jersey City, but it holds a lot of memories.

Jake was our engineer—the one responsible for recording us, mixing, and mastering our tracks. I didn't fully understand what his role entailed back then, but now that I'm an engineer myself, I have so much appreciation for him. When you think about it, Jake was the final touch, the one who crafted the sound we became known for. He was a critical part of the whole process, but I didn't see that at the time. Today, Jake is one of my mentors. I often go to him for feedback on my mixes and advice on equipment. He went on to have an incredibly successful career as a mix engineer, working with some of the biggest names in the Latin music scene, like Marc Anthony, Sergio George, Prince Royce, and the late Celia Cruz, among many others.

After recording with Jimba, our production team started shopping us to labels. But one thing kept coming up—our image. Without Roman to hold us accountable, we had let ourselves go a little. We were so focused on making music that we didn't spend enough time on our image, staying in shape, or promoting ourselves. Our production team did their job, but we fell short. I was the driving force behind the group at the time, literally, driving the guys to and from sessions, rehearsals, photoshoots, and shows, but I began to realize that the hunger we had as Strange WayZ wasn't there in ForeKast. We were content with being "studio rats."

Fredo was more interested in producing than performing. We practically had to drag him out of the studio just to grab lunch together, kicking and screaming. ForeKast kept recording, but we weren't gaining traction. I don't think we ever took to the stage together or did any events—I really believe we lived only in the studio and our own rehearsals. This was during the time when home studios were becoming more popular. I remember building my first setup at home with a laptop and computer speakers, using Cool Edit Pro as my recording software. It wasn't great, but it allowed us to create rough demos and spark ideas. Fredo really thrived in this setup, churning out tons of demos for the group. It was his love for production that grew during this period, and it's where I started to find my love for the technical side of the music business—a love that would come to define my career later.

There was talk of going on tour with Mario, and we prepared our showtape for the road, but that opportunity fell through. That was the final straw for me. Tired of the stagnation, I made the hard decision to leave the group in late 2003. ForeKast continued without me for a while, but after several lineup changes, the group was dropped from the production deal, and eventually, it disbanded.

We lost touch with Jimba—or if I'm honest, he got too big to mess with us anymore. Our calls stopped being answered as he rocketed to super-stardom. It left us feeling a little salty because we had been there for him during his come-up when he didn't have food to eat or a place to stay. But that's the music business for you.

Even though it didn't end the way I hoped, I walked away from ForeKast with lifelong friends like Ray, Fredo, and Victor. The experience taught me a lot about the music business—it's not just about talent. It takes a village of people to guide you, push you, hold you accountable, and encourage you. We had the talent and the music, but we were missing everything else. That's a lesson I've carried with me ever since.

CHAPTER 6.
SEARCHING FOR BALANCE

I've been working on a digital course where I spend a good amount of time talking about the importance of balance—between your personal life and your music aspirations. I dive deep into how crucial it is to get buy-in from the ones you love, especially your partner, how to communicate effectively, and how to manage the financial cost of chasing your dreams while still keeping the lights on at home. On paper, it sounds great—like a recipe for success. But back then, it wasn't something I practiced. Not at all.

In my early career, balance was the furthest thing from my mind. I wasn't treating my music like a business, with clear goals and a plan to turn a profit. Instead, I was chasing fame and popularity, driven by the idea of becoming the next big thing rather than building a sustainable career. Looking back, it's clear how misguided I was. There wasn't a single time during my stint with On2, Strange WayZ or ForeKast when I walked away from a show with a paycheck. In fact, I spent more than I made. Studio sessions, rehearsal time, new clothes for appearances, photo shoots—it all added up. My mind was so wrapped up in trying to "make it" that I didn't realize how much I was sacrificing, or how much of a toll it was taking on my family.

Stardom was reachable, my dream set before my eyes for the taking, but what I didn't see was the weight that came with it—the responsibilities that didn't disappear just because I was chasing a dream. I was also a young husband and father, juggling a 9-to-5 job, a marriage, fatherhood, and my relentless pursuit of making it in the music industry. There's something intoxicating about the chase, the thrill of being on stage, the rush of a crowd, the attention that comes with being an artist. It consumed me, blurring the lines between what was important and what was fleeting.

The problem was that I treated my wife, like a spectator rather than a partner. She was there, watching me, supporting me in her own way, but I wasn't including her in the journey. I was making all the decisions—whether it was studio time, shows, or trips out of town—without ever considering her thoughts or feelings. I think, at the time, I convinced myself that I was doing it all for us, that the success I was chasing would eventually benefit her and our kids. But the reality was, I was doing it for me. It wasn't about us. It was about the adrenaline, the attention, and the dream I had been chasing since I was a kid.

In those days, I didn't know how to balance home and ambition. And the truth is, I didn't try very hard to figure it out. But time is a funny thing—it doesn't wait for you to figure things out. And while I was out chasing stages, the world back home kept moving. My marriage was suffering, my kids were growing up, and I was too caught up in my dreams to notice.

It wasn't until later in my career—through trials and tribulations, through both great and rough times—that I learned a few key lessons. I discuss these in length in my course, but I want to share a few of them with you here. These insights have shaped not only my approach to the music industry, but to life itself.

Getting buy-in from the people you love, especially your partner, is essential when you're chasing a dream. The journey becomes much more rewarding when you share it together, turning individual ambitions into shared experiences. When your loved ones are invested, the struggles and triumphs are no longer yours alone—they become part of the journey, deepening the bond between you. It's no longer just your dream, it's our dream, and that makes all the difference.

Communication is at the heart of this shared vision. It's not just about expressing your goals but being clear and transparent about your progress, the challenges, and how your time is being spent. In a committed relationship, every decision you make—whether it's studio time or a gig—impacts both of you. Keeping your partner in the loop, sharing your schedule, and planning together helps prevent surprises and builds trust. When your loved ones are aware of what's happening, they feel involved rather than sidelined.

Financial decisions are another key area where communication is vital. Managing money while chasing a dream and supporting a family can be tricky. It's important to prioritize between what's necessary for your career and what can wait. In the beginning, I made a lot of mistakes—spending recklessly on things I thought were essential for my image. Now, I treat my career like a business, planning carefully, reinvesting wisely, and preparing for slow seasons. Discussing finances openly with your partner creates a sense of partnership, ensuring that both your dream and your family's well-being are supported.

By involving your loved ones in every aspect—whether it's sharing the dream, communicating clearly, or managing finances together—you create a solid foundation. It turns the dream from something that isolates you into something that strengthens your relationships and ensures everyone feels part of the journey.

There were also countless moments of joy and pride, especially when my wife managed to attend my shows. I vividly remember the glimmer of pride in her eyes as she watched me perform, and I could almost hear her sentiment echoing, "That's my man on that stage." Her support extended beyond mere presence—she would help me pick out outfits and even offered feedback on the groups look and image. In those moments, she wasn't just an onlooker; she was an integral part of my journey, sharing in both the highs and lows.

Those times when she was there meant everything to me. Seeing her in the crowd, cheering me on, made the experience all the more special. Even my children had the chance to witness their dad in action. I remember one particularly heartwarming instance when I took my son, who must have been around eight years old, to a photoshoot. While I was busy trying to strike a cool pose for the camera, he was contently riding his scooter around the set, lost in his own little world.

These glimpses of family life intertwined with my career were precious reminders of why I was working so hard, and they added a layer of personal fulfillment to my professional achievements.

In hindsight, I often wish I could go back and counsel my younger, more naive self. If only I had known then what I know now—how to balance ambition with the things that truly matter, how to involve the people I love in the journey instead of shutting them out. But you can't turn back time, and those lessons, as painful as they were, shaped me into who I am today. As one chapter of my life seemed to be unraveling, another opportunity was waiting on the horizon—one that would change everything.

Chapter 7.
Time for a Change

Leaving the Bronx wasn't just about geography—it felt like leaving a piece of myself behind. My wife had seen what I was too stubborn to admit: the path I was on wasn't sustainable, neither for my career nor for my family. The move to Orlando was her plea for change, a chance to rebuild from the ground up. I carried a heavy mix of resentment and hope, torn between the comfort of what I knew and the uncertainty of what lay ahead. But sometimes, the only way forward is to let go of where you've been. What I didn't realize then was that this move wasn't just a clean slate—it was a chance to rediscover not only my music but also myself.

It wasn't easy boarding that plane or saying goodbye to the life I had known for so long. The Bronx was more than just my home—it was a part of my identity. Every corner echoed with memories; every street had a familiar rhythm. As I stared out the plane window, watching the city disappear beneath me, I knew I was leaving behind more than just buildings. I didn't have a single friend or family member waiting for me in Florida. What I did have was a wife who loved me enough to fight for our future and children who needed me to be present—not just in body, but in spirit. She had moved down

49

with the kids two months earlier, settling near her parents in Orlando. After her second visit, she made a life-changing decision. I got the call while still in the Bronx: we were approved for an apartment. Her voice carried a sense of finality, a determination that left no room for hesitation. The message was clear—if I wanted to keep my family, I had to make the move. So, I moved.

In doing so, I left behind more than just a city—I left behind a dream. I said goodbye to the friends I had built my world around, to the opportunities I had worked tirelessly to create. It felt like I was closing the door on everything I had ever known. I resigned from my job, packed up what was left, sold what I could, and said my goodbyes. I wasn't just reuniting with my family; I was stepping into an unknown future. Music, which had once been my heartbeat, now seemed like a distant memory. I convinced myself I could find a new dream to chase, something more practical, more secure. At least, that's what I tried to believe.

Florida brought with it a great change—a needed change—and we adapted quickly. I found a job working for an airline, which came with one major perk: flying benefits. I took full advantage of those, making quick trips back to New York on weekends or even just for a night to see family. It was a welcomed escape, a brief return to the life I had left behind. My wife, children, and even my parents made the most of those travel benefits, and we flew often just to scratch that itch for home. But the reality was, we were working hard. My wife had taken a job at a daycare, our kids were adjusting to a new school, and I was pulling double shifts regularly just to make ends meet.

During this time, something unexpected happened: I rekindled my passion for writing—not songwriting, but blog writing. It became my outlet, my way of staying creative amidst the daily grind. I wrote about everything—life, family, the ups and downs of starting over. I would send my blog posts to my mom in New York, and she loved them. It made her feel connected to me, despite the thousand miles that separated us.

For a long time, music was the furthest thing from my mind. Living in our apartment, I had convinced myself that chapter of my life was closed. But as you might've guessed, it wasn't over. Not yet. And this time? This time, I thought it would be different.

In the spring of 2004, we moved from Orlando to the suburbs of Davenport, leaving behind the hustle and bustle of the city for the quiet of the country. Davenport was about 45 minutes away, and we were moving into a newly constructed house with a two-car garage. We now had space, a front and backyard—it was amazing. Coming from a fifth-floor Bronx walk-up, one-bedroom apartment to a three-bedroom, two-bath house with central AC was a dream. My in-laws had bought their home just across the street a few months earlier, so we had support. We were in love with our home, and our kids, for the first time in their lives, had their own bedrooms. It was great.

I'm not sure when it happened or how, but I started having an itch for music again. This time, I had no connections, no studio access, no musical friends to lean on—but I just had an itch. I missed it. Now, I was satisfied knowing that I didn't want to take the artist route—that was out of my system—but I still wanted to make music. By 2005, the digital music landscape had taken leaps and bounds in terms of access to the tools many major studios had for many years. Now, equipment like microphones and audio interfaces were more affordable. My wife reluctantly allowed me to set up a small desk in the garage where I had a laptop, a cheap dynamic mic, and a USB mixing board to record into. My first studio was born.

I wasn't looking to do anything serious like in my prior days; I just wanted a creative outlet. I reached out to a few producer friends in New York and started collecting beats—mostly hip hop and R&B—and I began writing and recording demos in my hot garage. Later, I ran into one of my friends who had also moved to Florida from New York. He was a rapper, and we connected, finding some solace in each other musically. He was in the same boat as I was, and we leaned on each other a lot. I started to do something I hadn't done before: recording another artist. I was channeling my inner Jake and starting to become an engineer and producer. Hmmm, well, this was new. As we got more serious, we began upgrading our gear, purchasing a condenser mic and getting some soundproofing. I quickly outgrew my space in the garage, and I'm not sure how, but I convinced my wife to let me move the studio to our bedroom.

Okay, I know what you're all thinking—what an asshole. How could I put my wife back in this position? Yes, you're right. I was selfish again, allowing my dream and passion to cloud my judgment, but let me explain. I really thought that my wife was no longer supportive of me as an artist, but in my mind, this wasn't that anymore. I was home doing music—no rehearsals, no traveling, no shows, no studio long nights—I was home with my family, but still doing what I loved. At least, that's what I really believed. The challenge became, when do I put the mic down? How do I separate music time from family time? That was always the challenge, and one that I failed miserably at. I was more controlled then because the studio was in our bedroom, and she was very particular about when that equipment had to be shut down. It was tough and was short-lived until we moved to our next home—game over! Lol.

We ended up moving to a home just a few houses over from our current one, but this home had four bedrooms and two and a half baths. It's so terrible when I think about it now, but guess which room was the first one furnished and moved into? Horrible, I know.

I finally had my dream studio. The upstairs bedroom was a dedicated studio space, and it was huge. I had a recording booth, a living room area with a projection TV on the wall—it was hooked up! In that studio, I really learned how to produce beats, record vocals, and mix songs. I had graduated from Cool Edit Pro to Nuendo 3, a much more robust digital audio workstation. I opened my studio to some of my friends who would travel from New York to visit us and record demos. One of those frequent visitors was one of my best friends, Ray from ForeKast. This is where he built his alter ego D*Rain, and we recorded so many songs. I started getting better and better at my craft and began recording my first mixtape.

One of my younger cousins, Tiffany, was an aspiring artist, and I ended up writing a few songs for her, so it made sense for her to fly down to me to record her project. I was finding my own way and discovering a new passion. I was very happy being on the creative and technical side now, with no desire to perform or be an artist. I lived in that studio, and my marriage paid a hefty price for it. I had it coming, I know.

Every few years, we moved as we searched for a home that was ours, and the studio lived in different places, upgrading each time. I grew as a producer and engineer and started working with more and more local artists, honing my craft and my sound. In one of my studios, I used to have a door that everyone signed, similar to what I saw when I performed at the Apollo. I still have that door today as a memento. There are a few names signed on that door of artists who are no longer with us, like Freddy "The Edit" Rivera and Joey from Marcy Place. One of the highlights of my career was having the legendary hip hop artist K-Solo work out of my studio. We broke night during that session and talked into the wee hours of the following morning. The more I worked with artists, the more I learned, and the better I became. It was in my third studio, where I lived the longest, that I had the most traffic and growth. This studio was located in my two-car garage. My two best friends helped me build it. We erected a room within the garage, built the frame, put up the drywall, and added an air conditioner. We built a custom desk and a recording booth, added lighting, and put in a futon. It was the place where Luis Marte Music Studios was born.

This is where I started to find my way back to the genre where I first got my start—Freestyle Dance music. This is where I developed the desire to re-enter the industry as an artist again. But this time, it would be different. It would be done my way, on my terms, and I would be the one driving every aspect of my artist career. This included recording my own vocals, doing my own backgrounds, mixing my own records, and being satisfied with being a non-performing artist. The timing allowed for it with digital music platforms on the rise, like Apple Music and Spotify. It was my turn, and I had some unfinished business and a huge chip on my shoulder.

CHAPTER 8.

REBORN

It had been a long time since I recorded a Freestyle Dance record, and as I considered diving back into the genre, I found myself grappling with a lot of questions. What did I want to sound like? What did I want to write about? Who could I partner with to help me find my musical identity again? The challenge wasn't just about making music—it was about reintroducing myself to a genre that once knew me as one of the members of On2. I had to figure out how to successfully rebrand myself, not only to the audience but also to the industry that had changed so much since I was last a part of it.

The Freestyle Dance music industry is a small, tightly-knit community that now mostly lives on social media—for better or worse, it's the audience we serve. It's a far cry from the heyday of the 1990s when Freestyle Dance was at its pinnacle. Back then, there was no social media as we know it today. Instead, fans and artists connected in more limited digital spaces like LaRoo's Chat Room, AOL, and various Freestyle Message Boards. These platforms were more about fan interaction than artist promotion, unless you were someone who straddled both worlds.

When I reentered the scene as an artist in 2012, the landscape had changed significantly. A few underground labels still existed, and only a handful were still putting out compilation albums. The genre had evolved, but a small group of dedicated Freestyle Music producers had kept it alive all this time. You see, Freestyle Dance music never truly stopped; it just shifted its presence online. Fans migrated to platforms like Facebook and YouTube, which became the new hubs for the genre's community (Instagram and TikTok hadn't yet come into prominence).

Despite the decline in mainstream attention, a few pillars in the Freestyle community managed to sustain their influence and maintain a presence. For instance, CPR's Clubhouse, based out of Springfield, MA, became one of the few places where you could still hear Freestyle on FM radio—especially the newer tracks from "New School" Freestyle artists.

Let me break down the distinction between Old School and New School Freestyle, because there are a lot of misconceptions out there. Old School Freestyle refers to the genre's birth and its most popular period, spanning from the late 1980s to the early 1990s. The artists and songs from this era are considered Old School because they dominated mainstream radio and enjoyed massive support from major clubs, record labels, and concert promoters.

As the early 1990s unfolded, Old School Freestyle began to lose its radio support. Around this time, a new wave of artists emerged, producing what we now call New School Freestyle. The key difference is that this new batch of artists didn't benefit from the same mainstream exposure. They weren't getting airplay on major radio stations, and they weren't booked in the big clubs or on high-profile concert lineups. They were essentially left to fend for themselves. I experienced this firsthand as a member of On2, where we were relegated to performing at smaller shows and venues with little to no radio play.

Over the years, the legacy of Old School Freestyle has only grown stronger—albeit not on mainstream radio, but in the concert circuit. Fans who grew up listening to the genre in the '80s and '90s, now in their late 40s and 50s, continue to clamor for live performances from their favorite legacy artists. These artists have built a loyal following that has stood the test of time.

Unfortunately, New School Freestyle has not enjoyed the same level of posthumous popularity. The genre's newer artists often struggle to draw the same crowds or command the same level of respect as their Old School counterparts. However, I firmly believe that New School Freestyle has single-handedly kept the genre alive over the years. Without the efforts of these artists, producers, and the community that supported them, Freestyle Dance music might have faded into obscurity.

There are always exceptions to the rules, and a few artists have managed to straddle both the Old School and New School eras of Freestyle. Artists like Willie Valentin, George Anthony, Peter Fontaine, Samuel, and Sammy Zone, to name a few, have successfully maintained a presence across both periods. These artists often still get booked on the bigger shows, sharing the stage with their Old School Freestyle counterparts. However, for most others in the New School scene, the reality is much harsher. The remedy for this has often been to create your own shows, book your own gigs, and rally your peers to bring this fanbase the music they love. It's tough, it's costly, and it's not always successful, but it's necessary.

These were the hard walls I ran into immediately when I decided to re-enter the genre. By 2012, the industry had become largely a social media game. To be successful, you had to be on the right side of the digital fence or, as my good friend Jose would say, have a song that was undeniable. In my eyes, I never really left the "industry." To be honest, I felt like I had much more success than most of my New School Freestyle counterparts. They weren't on national TV shows or performing in stadiums. I carried a huge chip on my shoulder and a bad taste in my mouth from my exit from the genre with On2.

Back then, I didn't feel like I was truly respected, or at least not in the way I believed I deserved. I was often overshadowed by my partner in On2, and people used to think that he carried the group and whatever nominal success we had. That narrative pissed me off, and it felt like the genre had turned its back on me just as much as I had on it. So when I made the decision to return, my mindset was clear: I was back and already earned my stripes. I was determined to be accepted as an equal off the bat, to demand the respect I believed I had earned based on my entire career. But to my surprise, no one really cared! Lol.

My first single, "I'll Be The One," did well and even appeared on NSR's (New School Royalty) Compilation Album – Volume 1. The track was produced by Phaze One, a talented producer who, like me, had stepped away from Freestyle for a time and made his return with this project. We collaborated again on my follow-up single the following year. I believed I had accomplished one of my goals: creating an "undeniable" song. Thankfully, it was well-received, but I quickly found myself dealing with a fractured industry, one that was divided into cliques—the haves and the have-nots. It was a harsh reality check. No one cared about Strange Wayz or ForeKast; to them, I was just Luis from On2, making a return after 15 years. I had to contend with old foes and demons—people who weren't eager to relinquish their status, or at least that's how I saw it at the time.

It took a few epic battles for me to realize that no one owed me anything. So, I stopped the chaos and focused on the one thing that really mattered: the music. I kept recording and releasing songs, one after the other, getting better and better with every release. My vocals became sharper, my writing more poignant, and I began to build a sound—a style—that was distinctly mine.

As I grew artistically, others began to take notice, and the calls started to come in. "Can you write a song for me?" "Can you produce my next single?" "Can I record my vocals with you?" "Can you mix my record?" It was amazing to witness how, with every release, I started to build clientele and eventually, a business. I fell in love with this new role. I was helping to mold and nurture other artists, and before long, even some of the Old School legends began reaching out to work on their projects.

Meanwhile, I continued exploring other genres, especially Bachata. I had the opportunity to work on a project for one of my old childhood friends who became a huge star in the Latin market, Toby Love. His first album was a collaboration of many old friends from our neighborhood who always shared a passion for music. Some of the songs that ended up on Toby's album were tracks we had worked on for years, finally coming to fruition. We spent countless hours in the studio back then, sharing writing ideas, never knowing what it would become. Toby made us all proud, and I'm grateful to have been part of that crew. This led to some work with the group Marcy Place, another Bachata staple group in the genre with hits like "Todo Lo Que Soy". They worked closely with Don Omar and came to me to record a comeback single "Donde Fue El Amor". It would be the last song Marcy Place would sing together with all three original members as Joey passed away two years later.

Since 2012, I have recorded and released over 20 singles under my artist name, Luis Marte (pronounced Mar-tay). I've also released several EPs, blending my passion for both Pop music and Freestyle Dance.

One of my proudest accomplishments is reuniting my old band, Strange WayZ, after 25 years. Since leaving New York in 2003, all the guys had started families of their own and also left the city. They eventually found their way further south to South Carolina, and at one point, all three of them lived near each other. We always kept in touch, but recently we had started talking seriously about recording together again. So, I organized a trip and ended up driving up to South Carolina with a mobile recording setup. That weekend was an absolute blast—we spent our time reminiscing about old stories, cracking jokes (what the older folks refer to as playing "the dozens"), and, of course, working on our first single together after 25 years. It had literally been that long since we were all in the same room together. I think we had a bit too much fun because I ended up having to make a second trip (this time flying) to re-record some vocals, but we did it. I went back to Florida, mixed the record, and we released it a few months later.

Let me share something about this experience that I think is relevant to this chapter and will be discussed more in depth in the next one. Strange WayZ never had the opportunity to release music commercially. We never had a record in stores, let alone on iTunes, which didn't even exist back then. The guys never had that experience, and I felt a responsibility to share that with them. Now that I had the capability, I wanted to make it happen—it was more important to me than ever. Whether the single was successful or not, it was an opportunity for the guys to leave a legacy. A legacy where their children and grandchildren, in whatever form digital music takes in the future, can look them up, play their music, and hear their voices long after we are gone. I already had that experience, and I felt it was my responsibility to give that to my three brothers.

We ended up recording two singles that are now available on all digital platforms. We rebranded ourselves as SWayZ, and our single "Let You Go" has done well. I'm incredibly grateful to the guys for believing in me and helping bring that project to life. We recently released a new single, which dropped just a few months before the writing of this book, entitled "She's The One," a record penned by Ray and I.

As an artist, I am content with where I've come from and where it has taken me. I don't see myself stopping as long as I have air in my lungs and can still hold a note, lol. But there's a new side of me that has taken on a life of its own, its own identity—still in music, but a new calling that goes beyond Luis Marte the artist.

CHAPTER 9.
BREAKTHROUGH

"You don't make music just to make it;
you make music to bring something to life."
~Quincy Jones

Transitioning from an artist to a songwriter-producer-engineer wasn't just a career shift—it was a transformation that reignited my passion for music in an entirely new way. As I moved away from the spotlight, only to return in a different capacity, I found immense fulfillment in the process of creating, shaping, and bringing other artists' visions to life. Building up my recording studio business became more than just a venture; it became a labor of love where I could mold talent into something truly extraordinary. I discovered a new sense of purpose in helping others find their voice, guiding them through the creative process, and producing music that resonated deeply with both the artists and their audiences.

Being an artist is not easy. It requires a willingness to expose yourself to critique and ridicule—a vulnerability that demands courage. I commend all those who take that plunge because when you have it, you have it, and when you nail that great song, the sky's the limit. But like anything in life, music is relative. Some will love your work, and others won't. What truly matters is how you feel about your creation.

The cardinal rule that has been instilled in me through all my years in the industry is this: you make music, first and foremost, for yourself.

It won't always be good, and that's okay. I have hard drives full of songs that will never see the light of day in their current form, not because they're bad, but because they just didn't work. Over time, I may revisit those files, pulling a line, a hook, or a melody that fits better in a new song. That's what music is all about—a feeling, a sensibility, a vibe. Sometimes it works, and sometimes it doesn't.

Over the years, I've learned not to be afraid or concerned with what the naysayers might think—they will always exist. But here's a hard truth: not everyone is an artist, and not everyone should be.

As a music producer and engineer, my job is to bring out the best in an artist's craft. I'm here to guide them, to provide a space where creativity can flow freely—and that's not always easy. I've had aspiring artists come through my door, some recording professionally for the first time, nervous and jittery, often with damaged confidence. Then there are those who have been through it before, who are well-rehearsed and breeze through their sessions. I learn immensely from both. My role is to nurture that creative process, to help them find that spark, and to craft something they can be proud of.

I'm not perfect, and I'm certainly no Quincy Jones, but I am confident in what I do know. My 30-year career in the music industry has prepared me for this moment, and yet, I remain a student of the craft, always learning and evolving. Every day, I continue to ask questions of my peers, study courses, and dive into YouTube tutorials to gain clarity on the things I need to master. You have to be willing to adapt because music is constantly changing and evolving. Software updates, new plugins, and applications hit the market daily—tools that can make what we do both easier and, at times, more challenging.

But that's the nature of this industry, and it's what keeps me engaged and passionate. The truth is, artists come to me for exactly that—my experience, my sound, my approach to writing, recording, mixing, and producing. When an artist chooses to work with me, it's their way of saying, "I believe in you enough to get me where I need to be." And I am deeply humbled and grateful for that trust. There's no greater fulfillment than knowing someone has placed their creative journey in your hands, believing that you can help bring their vision to life. It's a responsibility I don't take lightly, and it's what drives me to keep pushing, keep learning, and keep striving for excellence.

During one of these recording sessions a few years ago, I experienced something that has stayed with me ever since. I was working with an artist who had traveled all the way from Pennsylvania to record with me. He was shy and timid, clearly nervous about the process, but he had a friend with him for encouragement. His friend, an artist himself, had recommended that he come down to work with me, believing in my ability to bring out the best in him.

We dove into the session, tirelessly crafting his song. We re-recorded line after line, verse after verse, hook after hook, striving to get everything just right. Once we nailed the lead vocals, we moved on to adding the "color"—backgrounds, harmonies, and adlibs. The session stretched over several hours, but this artist was committed. He was open to trying new things, learning, and pushing himself beyond his comfort zone. At times, he was hard on himself, and I had to pull out every strategy in my tool belt to help him find the right vocal take.

By the end of our five-hour session, I could see the transformation in his eyes. There was a newfound confidence, a sense of accomplishment that hadn't been there before. I don't think anyone had ever dedicated that much effort to him or his sound before, and he seemed genuinely surprised and almost relieved by the outcome. As we wrapped up the session, I started to do a quick mix of the record while he was still in the room. He stood behind me, listening intently as I adjusted the levels and polished the track. When I finally turned around, I saw that he was sobbing. His friend was smiling, so I was momentarily confused. But then it hit me—his friend knew exactly what had just happened.

I asked him if he was okay, if anything was wrong. He looked at me, tears in his eyes, and said, "I never thought I could sound like that."

That moment wasn't about the magic of pushing buttons; it was about the magic of hard work, commitment, and believing in the process. It was a powerful reminder to me that at the end of the day, what truly matters is the dedication to your craft—whether as an artist or a recording engineer. That experience reaffirmed my belief that with the right mindset and perseverance, you can achieve things you never thought possible.

As I continued to build my business, Luis Marte Music Studios, I formed a new and valuable partnership with an incredibly talented individual known as DJ Merkone. Our first major collaboration was on what would become my most successful New School Freestyle record to date, "Apology IOU," released in 2020. The track garnered significant commercial success and was released on the 418 Music Record label to great fanfare. The project even featured the legendary Freestyle producer and mixer Carlos Berrios, one of my mentors and someone I often call upon for advice.

DJ Merkone and I have been working together ever since, forming a dynamic duo that is the driving force behind Luis Marte Music. Our formula is simple but effective: he produces the music, I write and mix the songs, and then he adds the final touches by mastering the record. It's a process that has brought us success over the past few years, and we're not planning to change it anytime soon.

A few years back, we received a call from another legend in the Freestyle world, one of the genre's pioneering songwriters, Andy "Panda" Tripoli. He was working on a top-secret project—returning to the genre as a songwriter, crafting new songs for his peers to help them make a comeback with fresh music. He chose us to produce and demo those songs, and it was an incredible honor to be in the same studio, let alone the same room, with the man who penned Freestyle hits like Nayobe's "Please Don't Go," Cover Girls' "Show Me," and TKA's "Scars of Love," to name a few. I was in the presence of Freestyle royalty.

One of the highlights of my career as a producer and songwriter has to be my work on a particular project that involved two legends—heroes of the Old School Freestyle era. I'm talking about TKA, the very group I mentioned in an earlier chapter. What made this project so special was that, although TKA had disbanded and reformed many years ago, these two members hadn't been in the same room together in over 30 years. I'm not going to delve into that part of the story here—because that's probably another book in itself—but I am happy to share the happy ending.

Artistically, they decided to reunite under a new brand called Aktual, a clever nod to their original band name. The most amazing part of this story is that after all these years, despite everything they had been through, the magic was still there. When they stepped into the studio together, it was like no time had passed. The chemistry, the energy, the creativity— it all came flooding back, and I was fortunate enough to be a part of it in a big way.

Through my relationship with Aby, it was a no-brainer for him to introduce me to the project, and Kay was open to it based on the co-sign. I have been writing for Aby for years, penning and producing a handful of successful songs, so when it came time to create the "Aktual" sound, I got the call and opportunity. Now, Kay was admittedly cautiously optimistic—you see, he wasn't really accustomed to turning over the reins to another songwriter to write songs for him to sing, so it took some convincing by Aby to give us the shot, and man, did we take the shot!

Now, before I get all "Behind the Music" on you, let me talk about the gravity of what was happening here. I had come full circle as an artist and now as a producer/songwriter. In the '90s, I was the one going to TKA shows and had to deal with my wife swooning over these guys as they lit up the stage singing hits like "Maria" and "Louder Than Love." I was the fan, and I looked up to these guys and, in many ways, emulated them as I built my own path as the artist I wanted to be. I had their CDs and cassette tapes carefully organized in my collection; these were some of my musical idols. But here I am now, being asked to write and produce probably one of the most important records in their career. I can't tell you how that feels, but I can explain how it happened.

Kay gave me a call, and we talked for a bit about what he wanted the "Aktual" sound to be. It was a mix of what K7's "Swing Batta Swing" sounded like and TKA's style, and he wanted guitars—he loves his guitars and needed guitars, lol. He sent me a reference of what he was talking about, and we took off running. I reached out to my partner DJ Merkone, and we started cooking up a beat. I think we nailed it on the first round because after sending the track to Kay and Aby, Kay called me back immediately. He only calls if it's bad news or great news, but we had a good feeling. The track was approved, and it was time for me to do my thing. I spent about a week recording the demo, going through several rewrites until I finally thought I had it. I had to play a delicate balancing act of writing for Aby's voice and range, which is pretty similar to mine, so that was easy, but writing for Kay was a little out of my range as he sings in a lower key. But I figured it out by listening to his older records.

I sent the demo.

"Don't Forsake Me" was released to great acclaim in 2021 and went on to be a number one record that year. I ended up winning a Songwriter of the Year award as well, and if you listen close enough, you'll hear me on background vocals. We are now working on the follow-up.

Dreams do come true.

CHAPTER 10.
A PATH FORWARD

As I reflect on the journey that has brought me to this point, I'm reminded of the countless challenges, triumphs, and lessons learned along the way. My story, like the music I've dedicated my life to, is one of evolution—marked by courage, struggle, and an unwavering commitment to moving forward. The path to realizing your dreams is rarely straightforward. It's a winding road filled with unexpected detours and tests of resolve, but it's also a road that leads to self-discovery, growth, and the fulfillment of a purpose that is uniquely yours.

My journey began as a young boy in the Bronx, where music was more than just a pastime—it was my lifeline. It was the escape from the challenges of urban life, the heartbeat of my dreams, and eventually, my calling. From the moment I first felt the pulse of Freestyle Dance music, I knew I had found something special. But the path wasn't easy. The Bronx was tough, and the music industry was even tougher. I faced challenges that would have made many people turn back, but I kept going. My journey took me from local gigs to national tours, from the spotlight as an artist to the producer's chair in the studio.

Perseverance has been the cornerstone of my journey. There were times when the road seemed too difficult, when the setbacks felt insurmountable, and when the dream appeared just out of reach. But each time, I found the strength to keep going. I kept writing, kept producing, and kept believing in the power of music to connect, heal, and inspire. This perseverance has allowed me to continue doing what I love, even when the odds were against me.

I discovered a deep love for the process of creating, shaping, and bringing music to life. Helping other artists achieve their dreams has become one of the most fulfilling aspects of my career. There's a different kind of satisfaction in supporting others, in knowing that you played a role in bringing their vision to life.

As I've grown in my career, I've also learned the importance of moving forward—not just in music, but in life. The music industry is constantly changing, and to succeed, you have to be willing to adapt, learn, and evolve. But growth isn't limited to staying relevant in your profession; it's about becoming a better person, a better husband, and a better father. Moving forward means making decisions that not only advance your career but also strengthen your family and your relationships.

In the early years, I often found myself so focused on chasing my dreams that I lost sight of what was most important—my family. The late nights in the studio, the endless rehearsals, the time spent away from home—it all took a toll. I wasn't always present, even when I was physically there. It took time and a lot of hard lessons to realize that success isn't just about achieving your personal goals; it's about balancing those goals with the needs of the people you love.

As I look to the future, I'm filled with excitement and anticipation. There's still so much I want to accomplish, so many dreams I have yet to pursue, and so many opportunities to make a difference. I'm committed to continuing my journey, growing as a producer, songwriter, and mentor, and helping others achieve their dreams. The projects I'm working on, the artists I'm collaborating with, and the music we're creating together all point to a bright future.

One project that I am particularly excited about is RBL. I formed a group with my two best friends, Ray formerly of ForeKast and Billy of Marcy Place. We have recorded our EP, and our first single release is scheduled for the Fall of 2024. Our recording sessions are so much fun, and I am reminded of how blessed I am to be surrounded by such great talent. These are type of artist who make me better, who challenge me to grow. I am super grateful and invite you to listen when you can. Our first single is entitled "Runaway" by RBL.

This book was something I have always dreamed of completing and here you are, reading it. We complete goals only if we set them. We reach success because we failed along the way. We do better, because we learned from our mistakes. I am committed to the work that's involved because nothing is easy, if it was then everyone would be an expert.

I am committed to my family, my marriage, my career; but above all, I'm committed to moving forward—no matter where the road takes me. The journey doesn't end here; it's just another step on the path forward. Take care of yourself and visit me sometime at www.LuisMarteMusic.com.

Made in the USA
Middletown, DE
03 November 2024

63803397R00044